Resin Jewelry Making

Designs, Techniques, and Projects for Every Skill Level

Regal Dekker
copyright@2024

Table of Content

CHAPTER 1
- History

CHAPTER 2
- Essential Tools And Materials
- Safety Precautions And Best Practices
- Setting Up The Workspace

CHAPTER 3
- Basic Techniques
- Advanced Techniques

CHAPTER 4
- Beginner Projects
- Simple Resin Pendant Necklace
- Resin Stud Earrings
- Resin Charm Bracelet
- Resin Keychain with Embedded Objects
- Resin Ring with Inlaid Design
- Resin Hair Clip with Embedded Flowers

CHAPTER 5
- Intermediate Projects
- Resin Geode Coasters
- Resin Wood and Resin Pendant
- Resin Flower Bangle Bracelet
- Resin Ocean Wave Earrings

CHAPTER 6
- Advanced Projects

Resin Wood Ring with Embedded Stones:

Resin Statement Necklace with Mixed Media

Resin Inlay Pendant with Metalworking

Resin Mosaic Cuff Bracelet

Resin Ocean Wave Ring with Embedded Sand and Shells

Resin Galaxy Pendant with Embedded Glitter and Stars

CHAPTER 7

Troubleshooting

General Tips

CONCLUSION

CHAPTER 1

Resin jewelry is a type of jewelry made using resin, a liquid plastic material that hardens into a clear, durable, and glossy finish when cured. Resin can be colored, tinted, or mixed with various additives like glitter, pigment powders, or metallic flakes to create unique and customizable designs. Resin jewelry can encompass a wide range of styles, from simple pendants and earrings to intricate pieces incorporating embedded objects, layers, and textures. It's a popular choice for crafters and jewelry makers due to its versatility, affordability, and the ability to achieve stunning results with relatively simple techniques.

History

The history of resin jewelry traces back centuries, with resin being used by ancient civilizations for various purposes, including adornment.

Ancient Times: Ancient Egyptians, Greeks, and Romans used resins like amber and tree sap to create jewelry and decorative objects. Amber, a fossilized resin, was particularly prized for its beauty and warmth.

Victorian Era: Resin gained popularity during the Victorian era, with the invention of gutta-percha, a natural latex derived from trees. Gutta-percha was used to make jewelry, particularly mourning jewelry, due to its black color and durability.

20th Century: In the mid-20th century, synthetic resins became widely available and were utilized in jewelry making. Resin casting techniques allowed artisans to embed objects, create layers, and experiment with colors and textures.

Contemporary Resurgence: Resin jewelry experienced a resurgence in popularity in recent decades, thanks to artists and designers exploring its creative possibilities. Modern resin jewelry makers often combine traditional techniques with contemporary aesthetics, resulting in a wide range of styles and designs.

Today, resin jewelry continues to evolve as artists experiment with new materials, techniques, and styles, making it a vibrant and dynamic medium in the world of jewelry making.

CHAPTER 2

Essential Tools And Materials

To create resin jewelry, you'll need a few essential tools and materials:

Resin: Choose a high-quality resin suitable for jewelry making. Opt for clear casting resin or epoxy resin, which cures to a durable and transparent finish.

Hardener: If you're using epoxy resin, you'll need a hardener to mix with the resin. Follow the manufacturer's instructions for the correct ratio.

Mixing Cups and Stirrers: Use disposable plastic or silicone cups for measuring and mixing resin and hardener. Wooden or plastic stirrers are ideal for mixing the components thoroughly.

Molds: Select molds in various shapes and sizes to create your jewelry pieces. Silicone molds are popular for resin casting due to their flexibility and ease of demolding.

Colorants: Add pigments, dyes, or alcohol inks to color your resin. Experiment with different colors to achieve your desired effects.

Embedding Objects: Consider embedding small objects such as flowers, leaves, beads, or charms into your resin pieces for added interest. Make sure the objects are fully dry and sealed to prevent them from reacting with the resin.

Release Agent: Use a mold release spray or powder to help release cured resin from molds more easily and prevent sticking.

Heat Gun or Torch: A heat gun or torch can help remove air bubbles trapped in the resin mixture, resulting in a smoother finish.

Protective Gear: Wear gloves, goggles, and a mask to protect yourself from resin fumes, skin irritation, and accidental splashes.

Work Surface: Use a flat, level surface covered with a disposable plastic sheet or silicone mat to protect your workspace from spills and drips.

Safety Precautions And Best Practices

Ventilation: Work in a well-ventilated area to minimize exposure to resin fumes. Open windows and doors, or use a ventilation fan to circulate air.

Personal Protective Equipment (PPE): Wear gloves, safety goggles, and a mask to protect your skin, eyes, and lungs from contact with resin, fumes, and airborne particles.

Read Instructions: Carefully read and follow the manufacturer's instructions for the resin and hardener you're using. Pay attention to mixing ratios, curing times, and safety guidelines.

Avoid Skin Contact: Avoid prolonged skin contact with uncured resin, as it can cause irritation or allergic reactions. If resin comes into contact with your skin, wash it off immediately with soap and water.

Protective Clothing: Wear old or protective clothing that you don't mind getting resin on. Consider wearing a disposable apron to protect your clothes from spills and drips.

Clean Work Area: Keep your work area clean and organized to minimize accidents and spills. Wipe up any spills or drips immediately with paper towels or a disposable cloth.

Mixing Precautions: Mix resin and hardener in a well-ventilated area and follow the recommended mixing ratios precisely. Use disposable measuring cups and stirrers to avoid contamination.

Avoid Heat Sources: Keep resin away from heat sources, sparks, or open flames, as it is flammable when uncured.

Dispose of Waste Properly: Dispose of leftover resin, mixing cups, and other waste materials according to local regulations. Avoid pouring resin into the drain to prevent potential pipe clogging.

Store Resin Safely: Store resin and hardener in a cool, dry place away from direct sunlight and heat sources. Ensure containers are securely sealed to prevent contamination and evaporation.

Setting Up The Workspace

Setting up a well-organized and safe workspace is crucial for resin jewelry making.

Choose a Well-Ventilated Area: Resin emits fumes during mixing and curing, so it's essential to work in a well-ventilated room. If possible, work near a window or use a fan to circulate air.

Cover Surfaces: Protect your work surface by covering it with a disposable plastic sheet or silicone mat. Resin spills and drips can be difficult to clean, so having a protective layer will make cleanup much easier.

Gather Necessary Tools and Materials: Collect all the tools and materials you'll need for your resin jewelry projects, including resin, hardener, molds, measuring cups, stirrers, inclusions, and protective gear.

Organize Supplies: Keep your supplies organized and within reach to streamline your workflow. Consider using containers, trays, or drawers to store and categorize your materials.

Set Up Mixing Station: Designate an area for mixing resin where you can work comfortably. Lay down disposable cups for measuring and mixing resin, and keep stirrers and other mixing tools nearby.

Protective Gear: Wear gloves, goggles, and a mask to protect yourself from exposure to resin fumes and skin contact. Prioritize safety when handling chemicals.

Ensure Adequate Lighting: Good lighting is essential for precision work. Make sure your workspace is well-lit, either with natural light or artificial lighting, to see details clearly.

Create a Clean Area for Curing: Designate a clean, undisturbed area where your resin jewelry pieces can cure. Make sure the temperature and humidity levels fall within the advised range to achieve optimal curing.

Keep Cleanup Supplies Handy: Have paper towels, rubbing alcohol, or resin cleaner on hand for quick cleanup of spills and drips. Prompt cleanup will prevent resin from hardening on surfaces.

Minimize Disturbances: Resin takes time to cure, so minimize disturbances in your workspace to prevent accidental bumps or spills. Keep pets and children away from your work area during the curing process.

CHAPTER 3

Basic Techniques
Mixing and Pouring Resin:

Step 1: Prepare Your Workspace

Arrange your workspace in a properly ventilated area.

Put on gloves, safety goggles, and a mask for protection.

Shield your workspace by laying a disposable plastic sheet or silicone mat over your work surface.

Step 2: Measure Resin and Hardener

Carefully measure the desired amount of resin and hardener according to the manufacturer's instructions.

Use separate disposable measuring cups for resin and hardener to avoid contamination.

Step 3: Mix Resin and Hardener

Pour the measured resin and hardener into a clean mixing cup.

Stir the mixture thoroughly with a plastic or wooden stirrer for about 2-3 minutes, scraping the sides and bottom of the cup to ensure thorough mixing.

Avoid stirring too vigorously to minimize the introduction of air bubbles.

Step 4: Add Colorants (Optional)

If desired, add pigment powders, liquid dyes, or alcohol inks to the resin mixture to achieve your desired color.

Stir the colorant into the resin mixture until evenly distributed.

Step 5: Remove Air Bubbles

To remove any air bubbles trapped in the resin mixture, gently pass a heat gun or torch over the surface of the mixture.

Move the heat source in a sweeping motion, holding it several inches above the surface, until the bubbles disappear.

Step 6: Pour Resin into Molds

Carefully pour the mixed resin into your prepared molds, filling them to the desired level.

Avoid overfilling the molds, as resin may overflow during curing.

Step 7: Cure Resin

Let the resin cure as per the guidelines provided by the manufacturer. This typically involves letting it sit undisturbed for 24-48 hours, depending on the type of resin and ambient temperature.

Step 8: Demold and Finish

Once the resin has fully cured, carefully remove the cured pieces from the molds.

Smooth out any rough edges or imperfections using fine-grit sandpaper.

Use a soft cloth to gently clean the pieces and remove any dust or debris.

Embedding Objects into Resin:

Step 1: Select Objects

Choose small objects such as dried flowers, charms, beads, or glitter to embed into your resin pieces.

Make sure the objects are clean, dry, and free from dust or debris.

Step 2: Prepare Molds

Arrange your selected objects in the bottom of your resin molds, arranging them in the desired arrangement.

If necessary, secure larger objects in place with a small amount of uncured resin.

Step 3: Mix Resin

Mix a small amount of resin according to the manufacturer's instructions, following the steps outlined in the previous technique.

Step 4: Pour Resin

Carefully pour the mixed resin over the embedded objects in the molds, covering them completely.

Use a toothpick or skewer to gently nudge any air bubbles to the surface and pop them.

Step 5: Cure Resin

Allow the resin to cure undisturbed for the recommended curing time, typically 24-48 hours.

Step 6: Demold and Finish

Once the resin has fully cured, carefully remove the cured pieces from the molds.

Smooth out any rough edges or imperfections using fine-grit sandpaper.

Use a soft cloth to gently clean the pieces and remove any dust or debris.

Creating Resin Pendant Necklace:

Step 1: Prepare Your Workspace

Set up your work area in a well-ventilated space and gather your materials.

Lay down a disposable plastic sheet or silicone mat to protect your work surface.

Step 2: Choose a Pendant Mold

Select a pendant mold in the shape and size you desire for your necklace.

Verify that the mold is clean and clear of any debris.

Step 3: Mix Resin

Measure the desired amount of resin and hardener according to the manufacturer's instructions.

Mix the resin and hardener thoroughly in a disposable mixing cup, following the steps outlined in the previous technique.

Step 4: Add Color (Optional)

If desired, add colorants or pigment powders to the resin mixture and stir until evenly combined.

Step 5: Pour Resin into Mold

Carefully pour the mixed resin into the pendant mold, filling it to the desired level.

Use a toothpick or skewer to gently nudge any air bubbles to the surface and pop them.

Step 6: Embed Objects (Optional)

If you want to embed objects, such as dried flowers or charms, into your pendant, arrange them in the resin before it cures.

Step 7: Add Bail or Hole (Optional)

If you want to hang your pendant from a necklace chain, insert a bail or create a hole at the top of the pendant using a toothpick or skewer before the resin cures.

Step 8: Cure Resin

Allow the resin to cure undisturbed in the mold for the recommended curing time.

Step 9: Demold and Finish

Once the resin has fully cured, carefully remove the cured pendant from the mold.

Sand any rough edges with fine-grit sandpaper, and clean the pendant with a soft cloth.

Step 10: Assemble Necklace

Attach the pendant to a necklace chain or cord of your choice to complete your resin pendant necklace.

Making Resin Earrings:

Step 1: Prepare Your Workspace

Set up your work area and gather your materials as outlined in the previous techniques.

Step 2: Choose Earring Molds

Select earring molds in the shapes and styles you desire for your earrings.

Ensure the molds are clean and free from any debris.

Step 3: Mix Resin

Measure and mix the resin and hardener following the steps outlined in the previous techniques.

Step 4: Add Color (Optional)

Add colorants or pigment powders to the resin mixture if desired.

Step 5: Pour Resin into Molds

Carefully pour the mixed resin into the earring molds, filling them to the desired level.

Step 6: Embed Objects (Optional)

If desired, embed small objects, such as beads or glitter, into the resin before it cures.

Step 7: Add Earring Hooks (Optional)

Insert earring hooks or posts into the resin-filled molds before the resin cures, ensuring they are positioned correctly for hanging.

Step 8: Cure Resin

Allow the resin to cure undisturbed in the molds for the recommended curing time.

Step 9: Demold and Finish

Once the resin has fully cured, carefully remove the cured earrings from the molds.

Sand any rough edges with fine-grit sandpaper, and clean the earrings with a soft cloth.

Step 10: Attach Earring Findings

Attach earring findings, such as jump rings and earring hooks, to the resin earrings to complete them.

Creating Resin Bracelets:

Step 1: Prepare Your Workspace

Set up your work area in a well-ventilated space and gather your materials.

Lay down a disposable plastic sheet or silicone mat to protect your work surface.

Step 2: Choose Bracelet Molds

Select bracelet molds in the size and style you desire for your bracelets.

Ensure the molds are clean and free from any debris.

Step 3: Mix Resin

Measure the desired amount of resin and hardener according to the manufacturer's instructions.

Mix the resin and hardener thoroughly in a disposable mixing cup, following the steps outlined in previous techniques.

Step 4: Add Color (Optional)

Add colorants or pigment powders to the resin mixture if desired.

Step 5: Pour Resin into Molds

Carefully pour the mixed resin into the bracelet molds, filling them to the desired level.

Use a toothpick or skewer to gently nudge any air bubbles to the surface and pop them.

Step 6: Embed Objects (Optional)

If desired, embed small objects, such as beads or charms, into the resin before it cures.

Step 7: Add Bracelet Fastenings (Optional)

If you want to add clasps or closures to your bracelets, insert them into the resin-filled molds before the resin cures, ensuring they are positioned correctly for attaching later.

Step 8: Cure Resin

Allow the resin to cure undisturbed in the molds for the recommended curing time.

Step 9: Demold and Finish

Once the resin has fully cured, carefully remove the cured bracelets from the molds.

Sand any rough edges with fine-grit sandpaper, and clean the bracelets with a soft cloth.

Step 10: Attach Fastenings (Optional)

Attach clasps, closures, or additional findings to the resin bracelets to complete them.

Making Resin Rings:

Step 1: Prepare Your Workspace

Set up your work area and gather your materials as outlined in previous techniques.

Step 2: Choose Ring Molds

Select ring molds in the sizes and styles you desire for your rings.

Ensure the molds are clean and free from any debris.

Step 3: Mix Resin

Measure and mix the resin and hardener following the steps outlined in previous techniques.

Step 4: Add Color (Optional)

Add colorants or pigment powders to the resin mixture if desired.

Step 5: Pour Resin into Molds

Carefully pour the mixed resin into the ring molds, filling them to the desired level.

Use a toothpick or skewer to gently nudge any air bubbles to the surface and pop them.

Step 6: Embed Objects (Optional)

If desired, embed small objects, such as gemstones or glitter, into the resin before it cures.

Step 7: Cure Resin

Allow the resin to cure undisturbed in the molds for the recommended curing time.

Step 8: Demold and Finish

Once the resin has fully cured, carefully remove the cured rings from the molds.

Sand any rough edges with fine-grit sandpaper, and clean the rings with a soft cloth.

Step 9: Size Rings (Optional)

If necessary, resize the rings to fit using ring mandrels or sizers.

Step 10: Polish and Buff (Optional)

Polish the resin rings with a soft cloth or polishing pad to achieve a glossy finish.

Advanced Techniques

Creating Resin Jewelry with Inclusions:

Step 1: Prepare Your Workspace

Set up your work area in a well-ventilated space and gather your materials.

Lay down a disposable plastic sheet or silicone mat to protect your work surface.

Step 2: Choose Your Inclusions

Select objects or materials to embed within the resin, such as dried flowers, leaves, small charms, beads, or metallic flakes.

Ensure the inclusions are clean, dry, and free from any dust or debris.

Step 3: Prepare Molds

Arrange your chosen inclusions within your resin molds in the desired arrangement.

Consider layering inclusions for added depth and interest.

Step 4: Mix Resin

Follow the manufacturer's instructions to measure and blend the resin and hardener accurately.

Mix the resin thoroughly in a disposable mixing cup, following the steps outlined in previous techniques.

Step 5: Add Color (Optional)

If desired, add colorants or pigment powders to the resin mixture and stir until evenly combined.

Step 6: Pour Resin into Molds

Carefully pour the mixed resin into the prepared molds, covering the inclusions completely.

Use a toothpick or skewer to gently nudge any air bubbles to the surface and pop them.

Step 7: Cure Resin

Allow the resin to cure undisturbed in the molds for the recommended curing time.

Step 8: Demold and Finish

Once the resin has fully cured, carefully remove the cured pieces from the molds.

Sand any rough edges with fine-grit sandpaper, and clean the pieces with a soft cloth.

Step 9: Polish and Buff (Optional)

Polish the resin jewelry pieces with a soft cloth or polishing pad to achieve a glossy finish.

Step 10: Assemble Jewelry

Assemble your resin jewelry pieces into finished items, such as pendants, earrings, or bracelets, by attaching findings or assembling components as desired.

Layering and Creating Resin Geodes:

Step 1: Prepare Your Workspace

Set up your work area in a well-ventilated space and gather your materials.

Lay down a disposable plastic sheet or silicone mat to protect your work surface.

Step 2: Choose Geode Molds

Select geode-shaped molds in the size and style you desire for your resin geodes.

Ensure the molds are clean and free from any debris.

Step 3: Prepare Base Layer

Mix a small amount of clear resin and pour it into the bottom of each mold to create a base layer.

Allow the resin to partially cure until it becomes tacky but not fully hardened.

Step 4: Add Color and Inclusions

Mix colored resin and pour it over the tacky base layer, creating swirls, patterns, or gradients as desired.

Drop inclusions such as metallic flakes, glitter, or small beads into the colored resin to add sparkle and texture.

Step 5: Create Texture and Depth

Use a toothpick or skewer to create texture and depth by dragging through the resin layers to create veins, lines, or patterns resembling natural geodes.

Step 6: Pour Final Clear Layer

Mix another batch of clear resin and pour it over the colored layers to encapsulate the inclusions and create a smooth, glossy surface.

Step 7: Add Crystals (Optional)

While the final clear layer is still tacky, insert small crystal or gemstone beads into the resin to mimic crystal formations within the geode.

Step 8: Cure Resin

Allow the resin to cure undisturbed in the molds for the recommended curing time.

Step 9: Demold and Finish

Once the resin has fully cured, carefully remove the cured geode pieces from the molds.

Sand any rough edges with fine-grit sandpaper, and clean the pieces with a soft cloth.

Step 10: Polish and Buff (Optional)

Polish the resin geodes with a soft cloth or polishing pad to achieve a glossy finish.

Creating Resin Jewelry with Inlay Designs:

Step 1: Prepare Your Workspace

Set up your work area in a well-ventilated space and gather your materials.

Lay down a disposable plastic sheet or silicone mat to protect your work surface.

Step 2: Choose Your Inlay Materials

Select materials such as crushed gemstones, metallic powders, or colored resin chips for your inlay designs.

Ensure the inlay materials are clean, dry, and finely ground for optimal results.

Step 3: Prepare Your Resin Base

Prepare a small quantity of clear resin following the guidelines provided by the manufacturer.

Pour the clear resin into your jewelry mold or onto a flat surface to create a base layer for your inlay design.

Step 4: Create Your Inlay Design

Carefully sprinkle or arrange your chosen inlay materials onto the tacky resin base, creating your desired design or pattern.

Use tweezers or a toothpick to adjust the placement of the inlay materials as needed.

Step 5: Encapsulate the Inlay

Mix another batch of clear resin and carefully pour it over the inlay design, ensuring that all inlay materials are fully covered.

Use a toothpick or skewer to gently press down any protruding inlay materials and remove air bubbles.

Step 6: Cure the Resin

Allow the resin to cure undisturbed in the mold or on the flat surface for the recommended curing time.

Step 7: Demold (if applicable) and Finish

Once the resin has fully cured, carefully remove the cured piece from the mold (if applicable).

Sand any rough edges with fine-grit sandpaper, and clean the piece with a soft cloth.

Step 8: Polish and Buff (Optional)

Polish the resin jewelry piece with a soft cloth or polishing pad to achieve a glossy finish.

Creating Resin Jewelry with Lamination Technique:

Step 1: Prepare Your Workspace

Set up your work area in a well-ventilated space and gather your materials.

Lay down a disposable plastic sheet or silicone mat to protect your work surface.

Step 2: Choose Your Materials

Select thin, lightweight materials such as paper, fabric, or dried flowers for lamination within the resin.

Ensure the materials are clean, dry, and suitable for use with resin.

Step 3: Prepare Your Resin Base

Prepare a small quantity of clear resin following the guidelines provided by the manufacturer.

Pour a thin layer of clear resin into your jewelry mold or onto a flat surface to create a base layer for your lamination.

Step 4: Arrange Your Materials

Arrange your chosen materials onto the tacky resin base in your desired design or pattern.

Layer the materials to create depth and visual interest.

Step 5: Encapsulate the Materials

Mix another batch of clear resin and carefully pour it over the arranged materials, ensuring they are fully covered.

Use a toothpick or skewer to gently press down any protruding materials and remove air bubbles.

Step 6: Cure the Resin

Allow the resin to cure undisturbed in the mold or on the flat surface for the recommended curing time.

Step 7: Demold (if applicable) and Finish

Once the resin has fully cured, carefully remove the cured piece from the mold (if applicable).

Sand any rough edges with fine-grit sandpaper, and clean the piece with a soft cloth.

Step 8: Polish and Buff (Optional)

Polish the resin jewelry piece with a soft cloth or polishing pad to achieve a glossy finish.

Resin Jewelry with Embedded Layers:

Step 1: Prepare Your Workspace

Set up your work area in a well-ventilated space and gather your materials.

Lay down a disposable plastic sheet or silicone mat to protect your work surface.

Step 2: Choose Your Materials

Select materials for embedding within layers of resin, such as dried flowers, metallic flakes, colored resin chips, or decorative elements.

Ensure the materials are clean, dry, and suitable for use with resin.

Step 3: Prepare Your Resin Base

Prepare a small quantity of clear resin following the guidelines provided by the manufacturer.

Pour a thin layer of clear resin into your jewelry mold or onto a flat surface to create a base layer for your embedded layers.

Step 4: Arrange Your First Layer

Arrange your chosen materials onto the tacky resin base in your desired design or pattern for the first layer.

Ensure the materials are evenly distributed and fully covered by the resin.

Step 5: Encapsulate the First Layer

Mix another batch of clear resin and carefully pour it over the arranged materials, ensuring they are fully covered and encapsulated.

Use a toothpick or skewer to gently press down any protruding materials and remove air bubbles.

Step 6: Repeat for Additional Layers

Repeat steps 3-5 to add additional layers of embedded materials, allowing each layer to partially cure before adding the next layer.

Experiment with different combinations of materials and layering techniques to create depth and visual interest.

Step 7: Cure the Resin

Allow the resin to cure undisturbed in the mold or on the flat surface for the recommended curing time.

Step 8: Demold (if applicable) and Finish

Once the resin has fully cured, carefully remove the cured piece from the mold (if applicable).

Sand any rough edges with fine-grit sandpaper, and clean the piece with a soft cloth.

Step 9: Polish and Buff (Optional)

Polish the resin jewelry piece with a soft cloth or polishing pad to achieve a glossy finish.

Resin Jewelry with Resin Casting and Carving:

Step 1: Prepare Your Workspace

Set up your work area in a well-ventilated space and gather your materials.

Lay down a disposable plastic sheet or silicone mat to protect your work surface.

Step 2: Prepare Your Resin Base

Prepare a small quantity of clear resin following the guidelines provided by the manufacturer.

Pour the clear resin into your jewelry mold to create a base for carving.

Step 3: Partially Cure the Resin

Allow the resin to partially cure until it reaches a gel-like consistency that is firm enough to carve but still soft enough to manipulate.

This typically takes a few hours, depending on the type of resin and ambient temperature.

Step 4: Carve Your Design

Use carving tools such as dental tools, X-Acto knives, or silicone shaping tools to carve your desired design into the partially cured resin.

Take your time and work slowly and carefully to achieve intricate details and smooth edges.

Step 5: Add Color (Optional)

If desired, add colorants or pigment powders to the carved areas of the resin to enhance the design.

Use a toothpick or small brush to apply the colorants evenly.

Step 6: Allow Full Curing

Allow the resin to fully cure undisturbed in the mold for the recommended curing time.

Step 7: Demold and Finish

Once the resin has fully cured, carefully remove the cured piece from the mold.

Sand any rough edges with fine-grit sandpaper, and clean the piece with a soft cloth.

Step 8: Polish and Buff (Optional)

Polish the resin jewelry piece with a soft cloth or polishing pad to achieve a glossy finish.

CHAPTER 4
Beginner Projects

Simple Resin Pendant Necklace

Materials Needed:

- Clear casting resin
- Resin hardener
- Pendant molds
- Disposable measuring cups and stirrers
- Small decorative elements (e.g., dried flowers, glitter, beads)
- Necklace chain or cord
- Protective gear (gloves, goggles, mask)

- Disposable plastic sheet or silicone mat for workspace protection

Instructions:

Prepare your workspace by covering it with a disposable plastic sheet or silicone mat.

Put on your protective gear (gloves, goggles, mask).

Measure and mix the clear casting resin and hardener according to the manufacturer's instructions in a disposable measuring cup.

Pour the resin mixture into your chosen pendant mold, filling it to the desired level.

Add small decorative elements, such as dried flowers or glitter, into the resin-filled mold.

Use a toothpick or skewer to adjust the position of the decorative elements and remove any air bubbles.

Allow the resin to cure undisturbed for the recommended curing time.

After curing, cautiously extract the pendant from the mold.

Attach the pendant to a necklace chain or cord to complete your necklace.

Clean up your workspace and store any leftover resin properly.

Resin Stud Earrings

Materials Needed:

- Clear casting resin
- Resin hardener
- Earring stud molds
- Disposable measuring cups and stirrers
- Small decorative elements (e.g., glitter, metallic flakes)
- Earring backs
- Protective gear (gloves, goggles, mask)

- Disposable plastic sheet or silicone mat for workspace protection

Instructions:

Prepare your workspace by covering it with a disposable plastic sheet or silicone mat.

Put on your protective gear (gloves, goggles, mask).

Measure and mix the clear casting resin and hardener according to the manufacturer's instructions in a disposable measuring cup.

Pour the resin mixture into your chosen earring stud molds, filling them to the top.

Add small decorative elements, such as glitter or metallic flakes, into the resin-filled molds.

Use a toothpick or skewer to adjust the position of the decorative elements and remove any air bubbles.

Allow the resin to cure undisturbed for the recommended curing time.

Once cured, carefully remove the earrings from the molds.

Attach earring backs to the resin studs to complete your earrings.

Clean up your workspace and store any leftover resin properly.

Resin Charm Bracelet

Materials Needed:

- Clear casting resin
- Resin hardener
- Silicone bracelet mold
- Disposable measuring cups and stirrers
- Small decorative elements (e.g., beads, charms, sequins)
- Bracelet findings (e.g., jump rings, lobster clasps)
- Protective gear (gloves, goggles, mask)

- Disposable plastic sheet or silicone mat for workspace protection

Instructions:

Prepare your workspace by covering it with a disposable plastic sheet or silicone mat.

Put on your protective gear (gloves, goggles, mask).

Measure and mix the clear casting resin and hardener according to the manufacturer's instructions in a disposable measuring cup.

Pour the resin mixture into the silicone bracelet mold, filling each cavity halfway.

Add small decorative elements, such as beads or charms, into each resin-filled cavity.

Pour additional resin mixture into the mold to cover the decorative elements completely.

Use a toothpick or skewer to adjust the position of the decorative elements and remove any air bubbles.

Allow the resin to cure undisturbed for the recommended curing time.

Once cured, carefully remove the resin charms from the mold.

Attach the resin charms to bracelet findings, such as jump rings and lobster clasps, to complete your charm bracelet.

Clean up your workspace and store any leftover resin properly.

Resin Keychain with Embedded Objects

Materials Needed:

- Clear casting resin
- Resin hardener
- Keychain mold or silicone mold with small cavities

- Disposable measuring cups and stirrers
- Small decorative objects (e.g., small toys, dried flowers, beads)
- Keychain rings
- Protective gear (gloves, goggles, mask)
- Disposable plastic sheet or silicone mat for workspace protection

Instructions:

Prepare your workspace by covering it with a disposable plastic sheet or silicone mat.

Put on your protective gear (gloves, goggles, mask).

Measure and mix the clear casting resin and hardener according to the manufacturer's instructions in a disposable measuring cup.

Pour a small amount of resin mixture into each cavity of the keychain mold.

Place small decorative objects, such as dried flowers or beads, into the resin-filled cavities.

Pour additional resin mixture over the embedded objects to cover them completely.

Use a toothpick or skewer to adjust the position of the embedded objects and remove any air bubbles.

Allow the resin to cure undisturbed for the recommended curing time.

Once cured, carefully remove the resin keychains from the mold.

Attach keychain rings to the resin pieces to complete your keychains.

Clean up your workspace and store any leftover resin properly.

Resin Ring with Inlaid Design

Materials Needed:
- Clear casting resin

- Resin hardener
- Ring mold
- Disposable measuring cups and stirrers
- Small decorative elements (e.g., glitter, small beads, metallic flakes)
- Protective gear (gloves, goggles, mask)
- Disposable plastic sheet or silicone mat for workspace protection

Instructions:

Prepare your workspace by covering it with a disposable plastic sheet or silicone mat.

Put on your protective gear (gloves, goggles, mask).

Measure and mix the clear casting resin and hardener according to the manufacturer's instructions in a disposable measuring cup.

Pour a small amount of resin mixture into the ring mold to create a base layer.

Arrange small decorative elements, such as glitter or beads, onto the tacky resin base in your desired design or pattern.

Pour additional resin mixture over the inlaid design to cover it completely.

Use a toothpick or skewer to adjust the position of the decorative elements and remove any air bubbles.

Allow the resin to cure undisturbed for the recommended curing time.

Once cured, carefully remove the resin ring from the mold.

Sand any rough edges with fine-grit sandpaper if needed.

Clean up your workspace and store any leftover resin properly.

Resin Hair Clip with Embedded Flowers

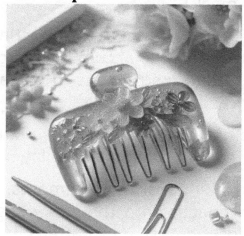

Materials Needed:
- Clear casting resin

- Resin hardener
- Hair clip mold
- Disposable measuring cups and stirrers
- Dried flowers or other small decorative elements
- Protective gear (gloves, goggles, mask)
- Disposable plastic sheet or silicone mat for workspace protection

Instructions:

Prepare your workspace by covering it with a disposable plastic sheet or silicone mat.

Put on your protective gear (gloves, goggles, mask).

Measure and mix the clear casting resin and hardener according to the manufacturer's instructions in a disposable measuring cup.

Pour a small amount of resin mixture into each cavity of the hair clip mold.

Place dried flowers or other small decorative elements into the resin-filled cavities.

Pour additional resin mixture over the embedded flowers to cover them completely.

Use a toothpick or skewer to adjust the position of the flowers and remove any air bubbles.

Allow the resin to cure undisturbed for the recommended curing time.

Once cured, carefully remove the resin hair clips from the mold.

Clean up your workspace and store any leftover resin properly.

CHAPTER 5
Intermediate Projects

Resin Geode Coasters

Materials Needed:

- Clear casting resin
- Resin hardener
- Geode coaster molds
- Disposable measuring cups and stirrers
- Various colored resin pigments or alcohol inks
- Metallic leaf flakes or powder
- Crushed glass or glitter
- Heat gun or torch

- Protective gear (gloves, goggles, mask)
- Disposable plastic sheet or silicone mat for workspace protection

Instructions:

Prepare your workspace by covering it with a disposable plastic sheet or silicone mat.

Put on your protective gear (gloves, goggles, mask).

Mix clear casting resin and hardener according to the manufacturer's instructions in a disposable measuring cup.

Divide the mixed resin into smaller cups and add resin pigments or alcohol inks to create desired colors.

Pour a small amount of clear resin into the geode coaster molds to create a base layer.

Utilize a heat gun or torch to eliminate any air bubbles trapped in the resin.

Pour colored resin into the molds, layering different colors to create depth and interest.

Add metallic leaf flakes, crushed glass, or glitter to the resin layers to mimic geode crystals.

Use a toothpick or skewer to create swirling patterns or texture in the resin.

Allow the resin to cure partially until it reaches a gel-like consistency.

Use a heat gun or torch to lightly heat the surface of the resin to create a smooth, glossy finish.

Allow the resin to cure completely according to the manufacturer's instructions.

Once cured, carefully remove the resin coasters from the molds.

Sand any rough edges with fine-grit sandpaper if needed.

Clean up your workspace and store any leftover resin properly.

Resin Wood and Resin Pendant

Materials Needed:

- Clear casting resin
- Resin hardener
- Wood slice or pendant blank
- Disposable measuring cups and stirrers
- Various colored resin pigments or alcohol inks
- Decorative elements (e.g., dried flowers, metallic flakes, beads)
- Jewelry findings (e.g., jump rings, necklace chain)
- Protective gear (gloves, goggles, mask)

- Disposable plastic sheet or silicone mat for workspace protection

Instructions:

Prepare your workspace by covering it with a disposable plastic sheet or silicone mat.

Put on your protective gear (gloves, goggles, mask).

Mix clear casting resin and hardener according to the manufacturer's instructions in a disposable measuring cup.

Pour a small amount of clear resin onto the wood slice or pendant blank to create a base layer.

Utilize a heat gun or torch to eliminate any air bubbles trapped in the resin.

Add colored resin pigments or alcohol inks to create desired colors, and pour them onto the wood slice in desired patterns or designs.

Use a toothpick or skewer to swirl the colors together and create marbled effects.

Embed decorative elements such as dried flowers, metallic flakes, or beads into the resin while it is still tacky.

Allow the resin to cure partially until it reaches a gel-like consistency.

Use a heat gun or torch to lightly heat the surface of the resin to create a smooth, glossy finish.

Once the resin is fully cured, attach jump rings to the pendant if desired and thread a necklace chain through the jump ring to complete the pendant.

Clean up your workspace and store any leftover resin properly.

Resin Flower Bangle Bracelet

Materials Needed:
- Clear casting resin

- Resin hardener
- Bangle bracelet mold
- Disposable measuring cups and stirrers
- Dried or pressed flowers
- Resin dye or alcohol ink (optional)
- Protective gear (gloves, goggles, mask)
- Disposable plastic sheet or silicone mat for workspace protection

Instructions:

Prepare your workspace by covering it with a disposable plastic sheet or silicone mat.

Put on your protective gear (gloves, goggles, mask).

Mix clear casting resin and hardener according to the manufacturer's instructions in a disposable measuring cup.

Pour a small amount of clear resin into the bangle bracelet mold to create a base layer.

Arrange dried or pressed flowers onto the resin base layer in your desired design.

Optional: Add resin dye or alcohol ink to the remaining resin mixture to create a colored background for the flowers.

Pour the colored resin mixture over the flowers and base layer, ensuring the flowers are fully covered.

Use a toothpick or skewer to adjust the position of the flowers and remove any air bubbles.

Allow the resin to cure undisturbed for the recommended curing time.

Once cured, carefully remove the resin bangle bracelet from the mold.

Sand any rough edges with fine-grit sandpaper if needed.

Clean up your workspace and store any leftover resin properly.

Resin Ocean Wave Earrings

Materials Needed:

- Clear casting resin
- Resin hardener
- Silicone earring mold (wave shape)
- Disposable measuring cups and stirrers
- Blue resin dye or alcohol ink
- White resin dye or alcohol ink
- Metallic leaf flakes or powder
- Earring hooks or studs
- Protective gear (gloves, goggles, mask)
- Disposable plastic sheet or silicone mat for workspace protection

Instructions:

Prepare your workspace by covering it with a disposable plastic sheet or silicone mat.

Put on your protective gear (gloves, goggles, mask).

Mix clear casting resin and hardener according to the manufacturer's instructions in a disposable measuring cup.

Divide the mixed resin into two cups.

Add blue resin dye or alcohol ink to one cup and white resin dye or alcohol ink to the other cup.

Pour a small amount of blue resin into the wave-shaped cavities of the silicone earring mold to create the base layer.

Use a toothpick or skewer to create swirling patterns in the blue resin to mimic ocean waves.

Allow the blue resin to partially cure until it reaches a gel-like consistency.

Pour a small amount of white resin over the partially cured blue resin to create the foam of the waves.

Use a toothpick or skewer to create texture and swirls in the white resin.

Sprinkle metallic leaf flakes or powder over the white resin to add shimmer and dimension.

Allow the resin to cure completely undisturbed for the recommended curing time.

Once cured, carefully remove the resin wave earrings from the mold.

Attach earring hooks or studs to the resin pieces to complete the earrings.

Clean up your workspace and store any leftover resin properly.

CHAPTER 6
Advanced Projects

Resin Wood Ring with Embedded Stones:

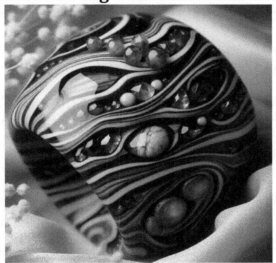

Materials Needed:

- Clear casting resin
- Resin hardener
- Wood ring blank or DIY wooden ring mold
- Disposable measuring cups and stirrers
- Small decorative stones or gemstones
- Sandpaper (various grits)
- Protective gear (gloves, goggles, mask)

- Disposable plastic sheet or silicone mat for workspace protection

Instructions:

Prepare your workspace by covering it with a disposable plastic sheet or silicone mat.

Put on your protective gear (gloves, goggles, mask).

If using a wood ring blank, shape and sand it to the desired size and shape. If using a DIY wooden ring mold, ensure it is properly sealed.

Mix clear casting resin and hardener according to the manufacturer's instructions in a disposable measuring cup.

Pour a small amount of resin into the wooden ring mold or onto the wood ring blank to create a base layer.

Allow the resin to partially cure until it reaches a gel-like consistency.

Arrange small decorative stones or gemstones onto the tacky resin base in your desired design.

Pour additional resin mixture over the embedded stones to cover them completely.

Use a toothpick or skewer to adjust the position of the stones and remove any air bubbles.

Allow the resin to cure completely undisturbed for the recommended curing time.

Once cured, carefully remove the resin ring from the mold or sand down any rough edges on the wood ring blank.

Sand the resin surface and wood ring to smooth out any imperfections and achieve the desired finish.

Clean up your workspace and store any leftover resin properly.

Resin Statement Necklace with Mixed Media

Materials Needed:

- Clear casting resin
- Resin hardener
- Silicone necklace mold or pendant molds
- Disposable measuring cups and stirrers
- Various decorative elements (e.g., dried flowers, beads, fabric scraps)
- Resin dye or alcohol ink
- Metallic leaf flakes or powder
- Jewelry findings (e.g., necklace chain, jump rings, lobster clasps)
- Protective gear (gloves, goggles, mask)
- Disposable plastic sheet or silicone mat for workspace protection

Instructions:

Prepare your workspace by covering it with a disposable plastic sheet or silicone mat.

Put on your protective gear (gloves, goggles, mask).

Mix clear casting resin and hardener according to the manufacturer's instructions in a disposable measuring cup.

Divide the mixed resin into smaller cups and add resin dye or alcohol ink to create desired colors.

Pour a small amount of colored resin into each cavity of the silicone necklace mold or pendant molds to create base layers.

Arrange various decorative elements onto the tacky resin base layers in your desired design or pattern.

Pour additional resin mixture over the embedded elements to cover them completely.

Use a toothpick or skewer to adjust the position of the elements and remove any air bubbles.

Sprinkle metallic leaf flakes or powder over the resin to add shimmer and dimension.

Allow the resin to cure completely undisturbed for the recommended curing time.

Once cured, carefully remove the resin necklace or pendants from the mold.

Attach necklace chain and findings to complete the statement necklace.

Clean up your workspace and store any leftover resin properly.

Resin Inlay Pendant with Metalworking

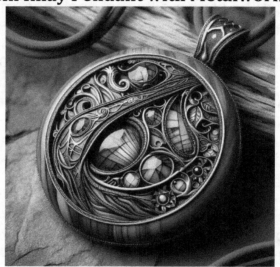

Materials Needed:

- Clear casting resin
- Resin hardener
- Pendant blank (e.g., metal bezel)
- Various decorative elements (e.g., crushed gemstones, metallic flakes, small beads)
- Metalworking tools (e.g., jeweler's saw, files, metal stamps)
- Jewelry findings (e.g., jump rings, necklace chain)

- Protective gear (gloves, goggles, mask)
- Disposable measuring cups and stirrers
- Disposable plastic sheet or silicone mat for workspace protection

Instructions:

Prepare your workspace by covering it with a disposable plastic sheet or silicone mat.

Put on your protective gear (gloves, goggles, mask).

Choose a pendant blank, such as a metal bezel, and prepare it according to your design preferences (e.g., shape, size).

Use metalworking tools to create intricate designs or patterns on the surface of the pendant blank.

Mix clear casting resin and hardener according to the manufacturer's instructions in a disposable measuring cup.

Pour a small amount of resin into the prepared pendant blank to create a base layer.

Arrange various decorative elements, such as crushed gemstones or metallic flakes, into the resin-filled pendant blank.

Use a toothpick or skewer to adjust the position of the elements and remove any air bubbles.

Pour additional resin mixture over the embedded elements to cover them completely.

Use metalworking tools to add additional details or textures to the resin surface if desired.

Allow the resin to cure completely undisturbed for the recommended curing time.

Once cured, carefully remove the resin pendant from the mold.

Attach jump rings and a necklace chain to complete the pendant.

Clean up your workspace and store any leftover resin properly.

Resin Mosaic Cuff Bracelet

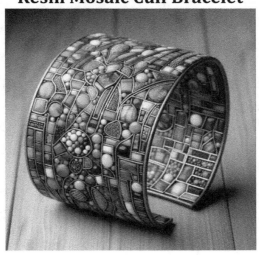

Materials Needed:

- Clear casting resin
- Resin hardener
- Cuff bracelet blank or silicone bracelet mold
- Various decorative elements (e.g., mosaic tiles, glass beads, ceramic pieces)
- Resin dye or alcohol ink (optional)
- Jewelry findings (e.g., jump rings, lobster clasp)
- Protective gear (gloves, goggles, mask)
- Disposable measuring cups and stirrers

- Disposable plastic sheet or silicone mat for workspace protection

Instructions:

Prepare your workspace by covering it with a disposable plastic sheet or silicone mat.

Put on your protective gear (gloves, goggles, mask).

Choose a cuff bracelet blank or prepare a silicone bracelet mold according to your desired size and shape.

Mix clear casting resin and hardener according to the manufacturer's instructions in a disposable measuring cup.

Pour a small amount of resin into the prepared cuff bracelet blank or silicone mold to create a base layer.

Arrange various decorative elements, such as mosaic tiles or glass beads, onto the tacky resin base in your desired design or pattern.

Optional: Add resin dye or alcohol ink to the remaining resin mixture to create a colored background for the decorative elements.

Pour the colored resin mixture over the embedded elements to cover them completely.

Use a toothpick or skewer to adjust the position of the elements and remove any air bubbles.

Allow the resin to cure completely undisturbed for the recommended curing time.

Once cured, carefully remove the resin cuff bracelet from the mold.

Attach jewelry findings, such as jump rings and a lobster clasp, to complete the bracelet.

Clean up your workspace and store any leftover resin properly.

Resin Ocean Wave Ring with Embedded Sand and Shells

Materials Needed:

- Clear casting resin
- Resin hardener
- Ring mold
- Disposable measuring cups and stirrers
- Fine sand
- Small seashells or shell fragments
- Resin dye or alcohol ink (blue and white)
- Metallic leaf flakes or powder
- Protective gear (gloves, goggles, mask)

- Disposable plastic sheet or silicone mat for workspace protection

Instructions:

Prepare your workspace by covering it with a disposable plastic sheet or silicone mat.

Put on your protective gear (gloves, goggles, mask).

Mix clear casting resin and hardener according to the manufacturer's instructions in a disposable measuring cup.

Pour a small amount of clear resin into the ring mold to create a base layer.

Sprinkle a thin layer of fine sand onto the tacky resin base.

Arrange small seashells or shell fragments onto the sand layer in your desired design.

Mix blue resin dye or alcohol ink into the remaining resin mixture to create a deep ocean blue color.

Pour the blue resin mixture over the embedded sand and shells, covering them completely.

Use a toothpick or skewer to adjust the position of the shells and remove any air bubbles.

Allow the resin to partially cure until it reaches a gel-like consistency.

Mix white resin dye or alcohol ink into a small amount of clear resin to create foamy white waves.

Pour the white resin mixture onto the partially cured blue resin, creating wave-like patterns.

Use a toothpick or skewer to manipulate the white resin to resemble crashing waves.

Sprinkle metallic leaf flakes or powder over the resin to add shimmer and dimension.

Allow the resin to cure completely undisturbed for the recommended curing time.

Once cured, carefully remove the resin ring from the mold.

Sand any rough edges with fine-grit sandpaper if needed.

Clean up your workspace and store any leftover resin properly.

Resin Galaxy Pendant with Embedded Glitter and Stars

Materials Needed:

- Clear casting resin
- Resin hardener
- Pendant mold
- Disposable measuring cups and stirrers
- Glitter (various colors and sizes)
- Star-shaped confetti or sequins
- Resin dye or alcohol ink (various colors)
- Glow-in-the-dark powder (optional)
- Protective gear (gloves, goggles, mask)

- Disposable plastic sheet or silicone mat for workspace protection

Instructions:

Prepare your workspace by covering it with a disposable plastic sheet or silicone mat.

Put on your protective gear (gloves, goggles, mask).

Mix clear casting resin and hardener according to the manufacturer's instructions in a disposable measuring cup.

Pour a small amount of clear resin into the pendant mold to create a base layer.

Sprinkle various colors and sizes of glitter onto the tacky resin base.

Add star-shaped confetti or sequins to mimic stars in the galaxy.

Mix resin dye or alcohol ink into the remaining resin mixture to create vibrant colors for the galaxy background.

Pour the colored resin mixture over the embedded glitter and stars, covering them completely.

Use a toothpick or skewer to adjust the position of the glitter and stars and remove any air bubbles.

Optional: Mix glow-in-the-dark powder into the colored resin mixture for added effect.

Allow the resin to cure completely undisturbed for the recommended curing time.

Once cured, carefully remove the resin pendant from the mold.

Clean up your workspace and store any leftover resin properly.

CHAPTER 7

Troubleshooting

Air Bubbles:

Problem: Air bubbles trapped in the resin can create unsightly holes or blemishes in your jewelry.

Solution:

Use a toothpick or skewer to pop large bubbles as soon as you pour the resin.

Use a heat gun or torch to gently heat the surface of the resin to help release trapped air bubbles.

Pour resin in thin layers to minimize the chance of air bubbles forming.

Cloudy or Hazy Finish:

Problem: Resin jewelry may sometimes cure with a cloudy or hazy appearance, obscuring the clarity of the piece.

Solution:

Ensure that you mix the resin and hardener thoroughly and according to the manufacturer's instructions.

Avoid mixing resin in humid or cold conditions, as this can affect the clarity of the final product.

Use a heat gun or torch to remove bubbles and help achieve a clear finish.

Sticky or Tacky Surface:

Problem: The surface of your resin jewelry remains sticky or tacky after curing.

Solution:

Check that you have mixed the resin and hardener in the correct ratio as specified by the manufacturer.

Ensure that you have allowed the resin to cure for the recommended amount of time.

Place the sticky jewelry in direct sunlight or under a UV lamp for additional curing.

Uneven Curing or Soft Spots:

Problem: Certain areas of your resin jewelry may remain soft or tacky even after curing, while other areas are fully cured.

Solution:

Ensure that you mix the resin and hardener thoroughly to achieve a uniform consistency.

Use a heat gun or torch to evenly distribute heat over the surface of the resin while curing.

Avoid pouring resin too thickly in one layer, as this can hinder proper curing.

Resin Leaking from Molds:

Problem: Resin may leak from molds, resulting in misshapen or uneven jewelry pieces.

Solution:

Use mold release spray or petroleum jelly to coat the inside of the mold before pouring resin.

Seal any cracks or gaps in the mold with modeling clay or tape to prevent leaks.

Pour resin slowly and carefully to minimize overflow.

Resin Not Setting:

Problem: The resin fails to set or cure properly, remaining soft and sticky even after extended curing time.

Solution:

Check the expiration date of your resin and hardener to ensure they are not expired.

Make sure that you have measured and mixed the resin and hardener accurately according to the manufacturer's instructions.

Ensure that the ambient temperature and humidity levels are within the recommended range for curing resin.

General Tips

Follow Manufacturer's Instructions: Always read and follow the instructions provided by the manufacturer of your resin and hardener. This includes proper mixing ratios, curing times, and safety precautions.

Wear Protective Gear: Protect yourself from harmful fumes and skin contact by wearing gloves, goggles, and a mask when working with resin.

Prepare Your Workspace: Cover your work area with a disposable plastic sheet or silicone mat to protect surfaces from resin spills and drips. Ensure good ventilation in the room where you're working.

Mix Thoroughly: Take your time to mix the resin and hardener thoroughly to avoid any uncured spots or tacky areas in your jewelry pieces.

Minimize Air Bubbles: To prevent air bubbles from forming in your resin, mix slowly and carefully, and use a heat gun or torch to remove any bubbles that rise to the surface.

Experiment with Inclusions: Get creative with inclusions like dried flowers, glitter, beads, or metallic flakes to add visual interest and texture to your resin jewelry pieces.

Layer Resin for Depth: Create depth and dimension in your jewelry by pouring resin in multiple layers, allowing each layer to cure before adding the next.

Use Molds and Bezels: Experiment with different molds and bezels to create various shapes and forms for your jewelry pieces. Silicone molds are great for intricate designs, while bezels offer a more customizable option.

Sand and Polish: After your resin has fully cured, sand any rough edges or imperfections with fine-grit sandpaper, then polish the surface to achieve a smooth, glossy finish.

Practice Patience: Resin jewelry making requires patience and attention to detail. Allow your resin pieces to cure fully before handling or wearing them to ensure durability and longevity.

Storage: Store your resin supplies in a cool, dry place away from direct sunlight to prolong their shelf life. Properly sealed containers will prevent moisture contamination.

Learn from Mistakes: Do not let mistakes or unsuccessful attempts discourage you. Use them as learning opportunities to improve your skills and techniques.

CONCLUSION

Resin jewelry making offers a versatile and creative outlet for expressing your unique style and personality. Whether you're a beginner just starting out or an experienced crafter looking to expand your skills, there are endless possibilities to explore in this craft.

From basic techniques like pouring resin into molds to more advanced methods like creating intricate designs with inlays and mixed media, resin jewelry making allows you to unleash your creativity and imagination.

By following safety precautions, experimenting with various materials and techniques, and learning from both successes and mistakes, you can create stunning and personalized resin jewelry pieces that are as unique as you are.

Enjoy the journey of resin jewelry making and the satisfaction of wearing or gifting your one-of-a-kind creations for years to come.